VOICES

The Root of My Rhyme

Ronald M. Baldwin Sr.

Published by Candy Publishing, LLC
www.candypublishing.net

Printed in the United States of America

ISBN: 978-0-692-86871-3

Cover Design, Reginald A. Cunningham

Photo Credits

Alonzo McNeal, Picture Perfect Photography
Deborah Shedrick, Shedrick Studio
Kendrick Thomas, Southshot Photography
Brooke Winn, Oh Beetlebum
Ronnie Phillips
Candy Productions

DEDICATION

I thank God for giving me these fiery words and visions to write this book. To my parents, Daniel J. and Betty L. Baldwin, Sr. (both deceased), I am forever thankful for your love, compassion, and sacrifices so freely given to me and my four brothers and four sisters.

To my wife Doretha Gail Baldwin, you have truly been a blessing to me while encouraging me through so much, thank you. To my sons and daughters, thank you for your prayers, love, and believing that Daddy would overcome.

Finally, to all the many people I met along my journey – your voices I heard within the depths of my soul although you never said a word. I heard you and now I speak for you, thank you.

TABLE OF CONTENTS

VOICES

The Root Of My Rhyme

Reviews

Congratulations, Ron Baldwin for this tremendous work. VOICES-The Root of My Rhyme is one of the most thought-provoking pieces ever written. After surveying some of the thoughts captured in this book, I knew Ron had penned a masterpiece. Get this project and read what these "Voices" are saying, it will surely bless your life.

Pastor Darold Montgomery
Life Changing Experience Worship Center, Pensacola Florida

VOICES - The Root of My Rhyme is piercing to the marrow of the bone giving the reader enlightenment, encouragement, and heartfelt words of fire and wisdom.

Min. Clinton Powell, Pensacola Florida

After mentoring Ronald for many years, VOICES is proof of the talent we knew he possessed from reading his other works. The writings are soul punching and earthy. Congratulations Ronald.

Kenneth and Vivian Reid, North Wales, PA

Very inspirational and eye opening, an excellent read.

Terrica Taylor, Pasadena, CA

Congratulations, Ronald Baldwin! I hope God continues blessing you in many ways as VOICES will bless many.

Greg Albritton, Atlanta Georgia

The controversial issues in VOICES will invite discussion and self-examination. Great poetic capture of his life.

Mrs. Georgia Blackmon, The Gathering Awareness and Book Center, Pensacola, FL

VOICES

The Root of My Rhyme

THE ROOT OF MY RHYME

I recall one particular evening, many years ago, feeling more alone than I'd ever felt in my life. I felt defeated and afraid, so I decided to rest and try to forget my negative thoughts. My thoughts took me down a journey of my past as I began to recap my life. I've experienced quite a few challenges and a few victories, but I found myself still wondering who I was. In my mind, I was somebody but to society I was nobody. I felt like a man lost inside himself without direction. For a few years, I served my country in the United States Army and later rejoined the civilian world and became a great car salesman.

Unfortunately, the success of being a convincing salesman led me down a reckless road of drugs, money, cars and power. Because of unwise choices, I was forced to live in hotels or with any family or friends who sympathized enough and took me in so I guess it's true to say I've been homeless, too. It didn't take long before I was fighting an addiction to the same drugs I once sold and secretly used. My secret became public and I was a common street addict like the ones I once drove by while shaking my head and feeling like I was on top of the world. Eventually my ex-wife left me and of course she took our children with her.

While having these recollections of my life, I fell into a deep sleep and heard voices speak to me from the many people I encountered throughout my life. Some of the voices I recognized and some I didn't. I heard cries of pain, moans from struggles, and deep desires to feel free, validated, and loved. I never had an outer body experience before, but there is no other way to describe what I went through that evening. I felt awake, but couldn't open my eyes. My room felt extremely warm and I slowly began feeling like my body was consumed by fire. Still dreaming, I felt the covers being lifted off me while what seemed like a ball of fire flashed past my bedroom door and down the hallway. I began to doubt that the out-of-body like occurrence was really happening. Was it all in my mind? Was I going crazy? Was I dreaming?

I decided to stop resisting the unusual experience and suddenly felt covered by a blanket of peace. The voices delivered a rapid flow of words that were coming too quickly to capture on paper. The voices, deep in my soul, were stirring to be heard. These were voices that were suppressed and kept silent throughout my life. Voices that needed to be heard. Voices from others that needed to be spoken. Voices full of passion and conviction. Voices that were going to change my life and free me and others. The voices were the beginning of my own Damascus Road experience – my journey to change from my previous life of drugs and crime.

As I slowly opened my eyes and reconnected to reality, I realized the flashing ball of fire I saw was a metaphor. – it was a personal light from Heaven giving me direction. I share these voices with you that will speak to you and for you. Voices you've probably heard, too. Some of the voices brought taunting truths of life – enlightening and edifying truths. Other voices came destroying what had been my own truth. The voices spoke boldly without reservation or boundaries. I share with you…VOICES.

Alonzo McNeal, Picture Perfect

It Matters

It should matter if we don't love and care for each other
It should matter when someone guns down another.

It should matter when we see the homeless on the street.
It should matter when we see people hungry with no food
to eat.

It should matter when we hear of those caught up in sex
slavery.
It should matter when a soldier dies for his bravery.

It should matter if a child is raised without a father.
It should matter when no one cares to bother.

It should matter whenever someone loses their life;
Does it matter if it is from a gun or by a knife?

Black lives, White lives, all lives matter!
We won't find any solutions with just lip chatter...
Let us not allow our hopes and dreams to shatter,
Because to some of us, **IT MATTERS!**

AMERICA'S FACES

America the Beautiful is what we are called.
But are we truly beautiful after all?
Look at the faces of the homeless throughout our nation;
Is there any beauty in their present situation?

Look at the faces of those in a life of abuse and prostitution,
They too are in search of a solution.
Look at the faces of the children born with a birth defect,
They are a group of faces that are on the verge of neglect.

America the Beautiful is what we are called,
But are we truly beautiful after all?
Look at the faces of those who kill innocent babies
Look at the faces of the physical and verbally abused ladies
Look at the faces of those who hate for the sake of their
beliefs and race.

Then you will have a true glimpse of America's Face.
Look at the faces of those who are left behind in education,
Living a life with little hope and no motivation.
Look at the faces of the drunk and homeless on the street
You can easily see their pain hidden far beneath.

America the Beautiful show your true face,
Stop pretending these things have not caused us disgrace.
The time has come for us to make these wrongs right
We must join together and continue in this fight.

Fighting to free the hearts and mind of every child,
woman, and man.
America the Beautiful let us lend them a helping hand
To help them in all possible cases,
Having one mission in mind to return hope to…
America's Faces.

Color Blind

The people of today must be determined to push
the racially divided past far from their heart and
mind. Forgetting the ways that were taught to only
love their own kind.

Black, Whites, Spanish and Asians, we are all the
same. We are all people of color and culture with a
different name.

Faced with an evil that has brought upon death,
hurt, and pain. To continue to live this way, we will
live our life in vain.

The problem of racism has always plagued man
from the beginning of creation. We have been faced
with this evil from generation to generation.

We are to love our brothers as we love our self
Remembering the example of love that our Creator
left.

We are living in a time that in one way or another,
Could cause us to lean and depend on each other.

Then we will discover that it is not determined by
the color of one's skin. It will be determined by the
kindness and love we possess within.

In times of unexpected trouble or sickness that
anyone of us could easily face, we would expect
someone to help regardless of his or her race.

A time when we will be thankful to find
The help of someone who is loving and kind.
A person that has managed to push away the
evilness of racism far from their heart and mind,

Someone that has truly become **Color Blind.**

Preach to Me!

I am feeling some kind of way today
Seeing so many of our children going astray.
I see the homeless young and old out in the cold
Huddled around an open fire,
With very little hope and desire
Preach To Me!

I passed by a woman holding close to her child
I could have sworn I heard their stomach growl
Evidence that they hadn't eaten in a while
Preach to Me!

As I turned the corner I see a mother standing and crying
Uncontrollable in the middle of the street, crying over her
child that lie dead beneath a crime scene sheet
Preach to Me!

Life speaks to us as we travel along our way

Let us help those who are in search of a place to stay

Feel their pain, it could be your blood running warm in their veins

Preach to Me!

They are in need of our love and care

Give them hope and whatever you choose to share

Then you can feel free to

Preach to Me!

My Scars

Each scar serves as a reminder of who and what I used to
be. Scars that no longer have the power to define me.
They are a road map to show me who I can become
In spite of all the wrong that I've done.

Things that has caused me shame over and over again
Things that taught me how to love myself and be a friend.

My scars I wear them proudly because they are life's
lessons. I look at my scars counting each one as a blessing.

They have taught me to never give in
And to always try and find ways in life to win.
A lesson that caused me to nurse my
Scars again and again.

Black Sheep

Black Sheep, why is it that you are always left standing alone? You are not an outcast, you have been one proven to be strong. Black Sheep, why have you been so badly talked about? Whenever your fellow sheep were in need It was you who they would search out.

Black Sheep, the world has tried to keep you from Holding your head up high.
Could it be they are ignorant to the facts and that's the reason why?

Black Sheep, you have been strong, the chosen one to lead The one that everyone thought would be the least likely to succeed. Black Sheep, you are indeed a special breed unlike all the rest Your purpose in life has always been to conform to Life's troublesome test.

Although you're called **The Black Sheep**
Throughout life's quest you have given us your very best.

Lost Inside

I am searching for myself looking inside
It seems that I am lost as I continue to hide,
Hiding from a world that has been so cold
I'm trying my best to hold on to my soul.

Lost inside of all life's fears
Feeling the pain I've had over the years,
Losing my place where I stood so firm
Wondering what happened and where I could turn.

I searched inside to find some form of light
Looking for the brightness of joy
Only to see the darkness of night,
Lost inside of myself who can ever find me
And who can ever reach me?

I creep outside of myself only when I'm alone
To see the little world that I call my own,
Only for that moment I am able to see
All of the things that I've **Lost Inside** of me.

Candy Productions

Memories

We became friends when we were both attending grade
school
Everyone would say that Mark was so cool.

He played sports and was very good in the game of
basketball
He signed a full scholarship to play at Seaton Hall.
After all, Mark stood seven feet tall.

In games my friend would often get hot,
Appearing calm as he post in position to shoot the game
winning shot.
Future hopes of success with plenty of money to spend,
Somehow he always managed to find a way to win.

There was another game that Mark played where he failed
to defeat,
A game he played on our city streets.

I remember the days that a number of coaches, family,
And friends were trying all they can,
But Mark wouldn't listen he wanted to be his own man.

It seemed as though he forgot about all those game
winning hugs,
Giving them up for a dangerous life of dealing drugs.

Now I can only cherish the short friendship with Mark
Sadly, one Friday night he was shot to death in our
community park.

No more plans for us to attend the same college and obtain
our degrees,
I am forced to go alone with only his **Memories**.

Racism

Racism is an evil that plagues every land
Once planted it seems to somehow expand.

Racism is a killer aimed to take your life
To snatch your hope and cut away your dreams like a
knife.

It is something about Racism that I can't figure out,
Where did this evil come from?
Why does it continue to shout?

Racism comes with its own agenda
To place fear in the mind of man
As though it was a plan.

I wish that someday it would die,
And stop causing so many of us to cry.

Cease from delivering its deadly pain
Leaving us with nothing in life to gain.
One day we will see that Racism has told us a lie
Then we can ask **Racism** why?

That Gun

That Gun has left behind miles of blood streams,
It has taken people's happiness, hope, and their dreams.

That Gun has destroyed countless lives around the world,
Just yesterday That Gun was used to kill a little girl.

That Gun has terrorized our children in school.
Are there any gun owners who think that's cool?

That Gun also killed an innocent old lady,
It has claimed the lives of a mother and her baby.

That Gun has caused division throughout our land,
We must put the weapon of love in our hand,
To stop That Gun from being used to kill our fellow man.

Something that we so often see,
That Gun could be used to kill you or me,
Yeah! **That Gun.**

Black On Black

Why is it so much Black on Black crime?
Have our struggles caused some of us to lose our mind?

Many Blacks around the world are under attack by their
own race. Killing each other at an alarming and steady
pace.

We are faced with all kinds of racially motivated attacks
To address these challenges we must first address this
very important fact - Blacks killing Blacks!

The struggles we have, they are great.
But we cannot allow these struggles to seal our fate.

We have witnessed a Black killed by someone who is
White, Oftentimes ignoring the many Blacks killed by
another Black the previous Night.

We march for justice and we call for peace;
When will the voices for the Black on Black killings be
released? A cry that calls for these killings to cease.

A Man's Tears

Sometimes in a man's life he hides his fears
Holding inside the pain and sorrow that would bring
about tears.

As he constantly tries to somehow be strong
The pressure of life just won't leave a man alone.

His love for life comes from family and friends
A man can then smile and joy blows like the wind
Once that love is lost, A Man's Tears suddenly fall
again.

It is not often that you see a man cry
Only when someone he loves suddenly dies.

A man was always told to hold back his tears,
Not to show his pain nor his fears.

Why is it so uncommon after all these years?
Society still doesn't expect to see **A Man's Tears.**

Candy Productions

I Need Thee

When I look at my life and I am happy as I can be

I need thee.

When everything is well and I look for others to tell

I need thee.

When sorrow comes I will cry out to you because

I need thee.

When I am weak I will call on the one who makes me strong

I need thee.

When my tears cease to pour and I can't cry anymore

I need thee.

It really does not matter where I may be, Lord always

I need thee.

Who is He?

The troubles of life overflowed me as water flows from a
cup. Those were the times in my life when I felt like
giving up.

During those times I felt a comfort of peace that overcame
me like the rising of the sun that glistens on the sea,
A man standing there with his arms reaching out to me.

I felt the presence of His love, peace, and care
As long as the man was standing there.

The feelings of joy suddenly increased
I felt my life with Him would never cease.

I stood thinking back on the times when I would cry,
He said, for those reasons I came to die.

No matter how tough it seems, this you must realize,
I will always be there to wipe the tears from your eyes.

Bottled Tears

As a child oftentimes over the years
I would bottle up my falling tears.

My tear bottle stayed close within my reach
To catch the tears that often rolled down my cheeks.

Whenever my spirit was low and I felt somewhat sad
I reached for my Bottled Tears and my heart felt glad.

Days when I was happy I keep my bottle near
To remind me of life's pains and fears.

I clearly remember the day that I lost my Bottled Tears
After I had kept them close for so many years.

The times of pain and sorrow was harder than any other
in my past. While searching for the bottle my tears poured
fast.

Exhausted, I fell into a deep sleep. There was a man
holding my bottle saying, these tears I will keep.

Never again did I have to bear life pains and fears;
Jesus bore them, when He held my **Bottled Tears.**

Alter Call

Can you hear the soft and gentle sound of His voice?
One that is pleading for you to change your life's course.

Have you considered whenever you began to cry,
The tears falling heavily and you not knowing the reason
why?

Can you feel the presence of His Spirit tugging at your
heart? The promises He made to give you a new start.

A feeling that is unlike any you have experienced before,
Could it be Jesus knocking at your heart once more?

Will you answer this voice that is offering you
unspeakable love? One that is as humble and pleasant as
doves flying above.

Will you continue to walk in your ungodly ways,
Having the hope of enjoying brighter days?

A kind of life that will cause you to stumble and fall,
Taking the risk to miss your last and final **Alter Call.**

Lord You Blessed Me

Lord you blessed me to see another day
When so many others have passed away.

Lord you blessed me to overcome my doubts and fears
You've never grown weary wiping away my tears.

Lord you blessed me to not carry envy or strife
Thank you for showing me the way to eternal life.

Lord you blessed me to have all that I own
My clothes, cars and a beautiful home.

None of this compares to the love that comes from you
Without that love what would I be able to do?

Miracles

Each day of our life there are many Miracles in sight
As we travel along our way, each miracle shines bright.

Many look to have a miracle someday,
Only to hear others thinking in the same way.

There are times that we see the lame begin to walk,
Other times we hear of the mute being able to talk.

We wonder in our mind, how could this possibly be,
Then we hear of someone blind, now able to see.

We see days when a doctor does all that he can,
The miracles we see are not in the doctor's hand.

The faith we have deep within
Is what heals our bodies so we may live again.

There will be times in life when one may doubt,
These are the times to see what miracles are all about.

The odds may be against you
But Jesus, the first miracle, will see you through.
Then you will realize, in **Miracles**, Jesus specializes.

Alonzo McNeal, Picture Perfect

What You Say

The words we speak have the power to shape the outcome of every situation. We must be careful when we are in need of any form of liberation.

The power of your words could hold you captive or set you free. Leaving you in a place you may or may not want to be.

You must be aware of the authority you release out of your mouth. It has the power to place you in a season of rain or a season of drought.

The words you speak will bring someone either life or death. You could be the one who builds their spiritual health.

Remember the words God spoke that created man, giving him authority over everything in the land.

You will be held accountable for the words you speak as you go on your way, words you will hear again on Judgment Day. So remember, watch **What You Say**.

My Angel Calling

While dreaming I see a face I don't recognize
Far from a distance, I see the beauty of her eyes.
She speaks softly as she draws near,
Motion in her lips but the words are not clear.

I remember the sun shining through the trees
I felt the wind blowing as it moved throughout the leaves.
I saw beautiful birds flying through the air
I remember the color of the woman's hair.

She showed me things of my past
So clear as if I was looking through a glass.
She brought me to a place so beautiful and bright
In the midst of a throne there was a face shining like the sunlight.

When I awaken all of my sickness was gone.
A body that was weak suddenly became strong.
My life has never been the same
I often hear **My Angel Calling** my name.

A Mother's Love

There is something about a mother's love that many may not understand. Her love is always unconditional looking for reasons to lend a helping hand. Love that has shaped cultures and impacted the lives of every woman and man.

She strengthens her children and encourages them to be strong. A mother will never leave her child to stand alone.

She serves as a friend and counselor against the many challenges life brings. Giving her child an emotional boost to accomplish their goals and dreams.

Regardless of the failures during the life journey of her child. She reflects back on the day that child made her smile.

Demonstrating a mother's love that has no limitations shows no form of a demeaning confrontation.
She possesses a kind of love that is unconditional.

Aimed to build a foundation of trust.
A kind of love that should be in the heart of all of us.

My Father

My Father is someone who is special in so many ways.
He seems to make it through the roughest days.

He seems firm and hard in his own way,
But many late nights I would often hear my father pray.

The love of my father is difficult to explain
He protects his family from hurt and shame.
He does so many things to protect our family's name.

A father is the beginning of any man's life,
He has love and compassion for his kids and his wife.

The love of my father continues to grow,
The distance of that love no one will ever know.

When our family is weak our father is always strong,
His desire for his children is for them to get along.

Words of advice he has always been willing to share
When times get hard he is the first to be there;
Why? Because he is My Father and I know he cares.

Mother's Cry

We often show a great love for our mother,
A kind of love that is stronger than any other.

We say, for her we would die.
Then why do we make our mother's cry?

We live our lives in our own way,
Sometimes we never stop to listen to what our mothers
have to say.

But while we live our lives and blessings come
our way, just remember for her children a mother will
pray.

So during your day as time passes by,
Call up your mother and say hi.

You never know how long she will be here,
Just show your mother to you she is dear.

Because it will become a day that your mother will die,
In that grave your precious mother will lie.

You will then search your heart and mind for the reasons
Why, maybe it's only because we made our **Mother's Cry.**

God Knows

God's eyes constantly roam throughout the earth
He knows the things we need far before our birth.

Our needs and desires are already met
Although we have not asked Him yet.

We may get hit by life's challenging blows
Don't get discouraged because God already knows.

He knows when the earth needs rain;
He knows whenever your body is in pain.

He knows about your sins and your confessions;
He is now positioning you for **His favor and His blessings.**

RONALD M. BALDWIN

The Silent Cry of a Baby

For years around the world the helpless and innocent cry
But only a few are truly concerned about the reasons why.

They are small, even smaller than what the naked eye can
see, millions are being killed. It could have easily been you
or me.

Their cries are coming from the inside out
It's a wonder they have not been heard;
How loud do we expect these babies to shout?

A decision is made to end their innocent lives
That no longer use the cutting of surgeons' knives.

Ending the life of what could have been a beautiful boy or
girl, It makes you wonder what has happened in the hearts
of some of the women of our world.

How can someone be so brutal and cold?
Destroying what has already become a living soul
To make "that choice" can cause shame and disgrace
Something in life that many have faced.

To intentionally kill one of His innocent babies
Then pretend that it's common among our society of
ladies.

Let us all put a stop to these cruel acts. It is one of many
ways that these babies are under attack.

Let us learn to be compassionate and listen for their
innocent cry. Help stop the record number of these babies
that innocently die.

Encourage a woman to stand up and give birth
and be a God-fearing lady…one who has heard
The Silent Cry of a Baby.

ME

Happy moving like the waves on the sea
Watching, waiting as patient as I can be.

Running and jumping for joy
Thinking of the times when I was a little boy.

Living and searching for a better life
There are moments of sadness and strife.

Hoping this journey will lead me far away
From the things I am faced to see each day.

Where should I go? What shall I do?
Who can I call on to help me make it through?

Where are the answers to my many questions?
Why am I lost with no one to give me directions?

Desiring for a day when I will become free
Still, I find myself in search of **ME**.

Candy Productions

Lost Within

I search inside myself to discover who I am
I find only that which I have become.

Not understanding all the reasons why
The tears begin to flow from my eyes.

Lost within myself, feeling that nothing is left
I know my life is worth living
Where should I begin to start forgiving.

Forgiving myself for all I've allowed myself to become
With thoughts that cause my whole body to feel numb.

Feelings of losing myself each day that goes by
I find myself looking up towards the sky.

Why am I feeling this way?
How will I be able to find the right words to say?

After I've caused so many people great pain,
Am I living my life in vain?

I hope and believe that these feelings will one day change,
As I search to find ways to remain sane.

Maybe these thoughts and feelings have no end,
As I continue to search for the man **Lost Within**.

Listen

Listen as the birds sing their song
Listen to the children crying out for their mom.

Listen to the voice that speaks softly inside
Pleading with you to tell the truth, but instead you lied.

Listen to the sound of the violence everywhere
Listen to the babies dying as if no one cares.

Listen to the wind as it blows its way
Listen to the voices of the children who've gone astray.

Listen to the men who are locked inside a cell
It makes you wonder if we are living on earth, or is this hell.

The answer lies inside each of us,
Let us stop to hear their soft voice... **Listen!**

I Find Myself

I find myself alone gazing into the sky
Questioning myself and wondering why.

Why have I caused so much self-inflicted pain
As I search for ways to somehow maintain.

I search to find my way out of this horrible maze
Feeling as though I am stuck in a daze.

Dazed to a life that could be filled with happiness and hope
Determined to find a better way for me to cope.

After all, what in life do I have left,
 If I give up the search to find myself?

SEARCH

Another day has come and the internal search has begun
A search to find (me) that lost one.

I find myself looking deep within
A very lonely place is where my search began.

Clearly, I see the roads of life I've often traveled
The memories of many events seem hard to unravel.

Finding a heart that is filled with commotion,
Unable to control the waves of my emotions.

Something that forever weighs heavily on my mind,
As I continue my search for the person I'm trying to
Find.

Slow Down

Feeling the wind blowing upon my face
As I walked along at a very fast pace.

So many thoughts running through my mind,
The answers to these thoughts I cannot find.

It seemed that everyone was moving in slow motion,
The look on their faces gave me that notion.

What could possibly lie ahead?
I began to feel somewhat funny inside,
But I continued to walk, keeping my fast stride.

As I reached the corner to cross the street
A fast moving car barely missed my feet.

I saw my life flash before my eyes,
Then I realized,
 I better **Slow Down**.

Be Endless

Each day we live, our soul search for its permanent place of rest.

The challenges of life often put us through the test.

Challenging us to choose whether or not...

Life could be endless...
Dreams could be endless...
Love could be endless...
Hope could be endless...
Joy could be endless...
Peace could be endless...

Your desire for them all should forever **Be Endless.**

Southshot Photography

Lost Child

They are innocent and sweet often making us smile
Many of us haven't seen them in a while.
Our hearts and minds search for their little souls
Asking others, but no one really knows.

We experience days of rain and of sunshine
We always have the Lost Child on our mind.
Living with the fear of what could possibly be,
As we find ourselves falling to our knees.

Praying for those who are experiencing this pain
Oftentimes not knowing their names.
The hope we have is not always clear
As we closely watch our child we hold near.

Sometimes our hearts are sadly broken
Remembering the last words the lost child spoken.
Then we learn that another child was killed,
We can only imagine how their parents must feel.

When a little child is placed into the ground
Let us not forget the many others who have not been
found as our hopeful search begins for another
Lost Child.

Candy Productions

Grayest American Day
09/11

The day that will forever be a part of many American's
mind, as we search for answers of some kind.

A horrible dreadful day of smoke, fire and alarm,
In a "Mighty Nation" whose borders were to be safe and
calm.

A day when the world merchants had a reason to cry
Watching the fire and smoke from the Trade Towers
ascending into the sky.

A day of sadness and distress, a day of waste, desolation
and gloominess. When the skies of two historic cities were
filled with darkness.

The day when the trumpet and alarms continued to sound,
When the "World Wonder" towers came crashing to the
ground.

Sadness, madness, and revenge were visible on faces
everywhere. There was not an American heart that was
not filled with compassion and care. While they witnessed
the distress upon the faces of everyone.

All wondering who and how this could have been done.

The presence of horror, blood, pain and death stood out before our Nation's eyes. Watching the brave and relentless sacrifices of many came as no surprise.

There were those who could only be of help in the most common way, as many families, men, women, and children gathered together to pray. Praying for the lives of those we lost on this **Grayest American Day**.

Candy Productions

Veteran's Cry

Many Veterans have died in honor of our Freedom Flag
Rarely do we know the name listed on the dog tag.

We see them with a missing arm or leg.
Sadly, some are on the street corner having to beg.

They fought for the freedom of our great land.
Why is it so hard for some people to understand?
They are in need of our helping hand.

Some were blessed to evade an enemy that fiercely
Aimed to take away their soul,
Only to come back home to be treated so distant and cold.

We must honor and hear every Veteran's Cry.
 We all should be able to identify the reasons why.
Are there any bombs raining down on you from the sky?

Dedicated to our American Veterans and those lost in combat

WAR

The presence of war is heard all across our land.
Wars are being fought in the hearts and minds of man.

War is cruel and it brings about fear,
We wonder why wars kill so many that we hold dear.

As we search for peace in our land and in our minds
Why are words of war constantly in the headlines?

Mothers and fathers see their sons and daughters going
off to war. They can barely stand still as their tears
began to pour.

What can we do about this killer of millions?
Why are the world governments still spending billions?

Is it because of their continual greed for wealth in the land,
Or could it be the wars that are being fought
Inside the minds of man?

War Zone

Where has our nation's freedom gone?
It feels like we are all living in a war zone.

We are living our lives in constant fear everyday
Hoping that we are not killed in an awful way.

Threats are being heard from groups all around the world
Through television, social media and our cell phones,
While our city streets are compared to war zones.

Wars are being fought in our streets in order to
survive, with one mission in mind to try and stay
alive.

Kill or be killed one or the other,
Someone just witnessed the killing of their brother.

What happened to the peace and freedom we once shared?
Today, people everywhere are downright scared.

We could be caught in the path of gun violence
As we travel on our way home.

Violence that will trap us in the middle of a deadly
War Zone.

Fallen Heros

Dedicated to the fallen U.S. Service Men and Women

All of their names we may never really know,
They are courageous and brave like any well-known hero.

Determined to fight for the freedom of you and I.
Brave men and women who are not afraid to die.

They are people from your city or town
Fearless as they enter the enemies' battle ground.

They go into battle protecting us without knowing our
race or name, fighting for freedom, not for glory or fame.

Often faced with many dangerous missions
Putting themselves in life threatening positions.

Men and Women who are Fallen Heroes
Some we will never have the pleasure to know.

Fallen Heroes who were born to be brave,
Who have proven their love for freedom to the grave.

UNTOLD

I am listening to a familiar voice that oftentimes speaks to my soul, speaking words that will never be told.

I find myself in a motionless state,
Fully unable to communicate.

The voice asks questions that clearly pertain to my life,
Questions that cut deep into my soul like a knife.

I feel my body getting cold,
I listen as the voice began to take hold.

Cautioning me to never unfold
The warm words that "He" spoke into my soul,
Words that will forever remain **Untold.**

In Cold Blood

There are those in authority who abuse their
power. Taking away our lives and dreams each and
every hour.

They are abusive physically and mentally, as they
hide behind their positions some never to face their
penalty.

They surround themselves with people of the same
mind, constantly covering up the evidence of all
their crimes.

They appear to be somewhat kind, but their hatred
and corruption is concealed inside their mind.

Their victims could easily be you or I
By the hands of these people any one of us can die.

It really does not matter if you are a woman or a
man, your blood can one day be found on their
hand.

Some of us may feel that these actions are directed
Towards a particular race. Until it happens to
someone we love, directly in front of our face.

It is happening to us all each and everyday.
Are you going to continue to let them have their
way?

Or, will you wait to be struck by this deadly club,
Taking the chance to be killed **In Cold Blood!**

Judgment Day

There will come a time when you will no longer have the
last word to say.
A time when you won't have any bills to pay.

When Earth and The Heavens will flee away, that time
is Judgment Day.

A day when there will be no place to hide.
A day that will reveal the truth every time you lied.

A day the rich, poor, small, and great will stand before His
throne.
Remember, Jesus said He would never leave you alone.

The day when "The Books" will finally be open,
Revealing your darkest secrets and every word you have
spoken.

A time that will display every choice you've made in life,
How you've treated your fellow man, your children, your
husband or wife.

A time when joy is mixed with much sorrow,
Sadly, for some there will be no brighter tomorrow.

The dead in the sea will stand before His throne
To receive His judgment and their eternal home.

Be encouraged if you are living the Godly way,
Treating people with love and respect each passing day.

Everything we have done from the time of our birth
Is recorded until the very moment we leave this earth.

Watch what you do and be careful what you say,
Because the whole world will find out on
Judgment Day.

Fancy Dancer

The nightlife is the life he has always lived for
Looking forward to entering into the night club's door.

With an energy that constantly began to soar
Whenever he visionS himself dancing across the floor.

The club is packed from wall to wall. Ladies whispering
about the dancer that is handsome and tall.

Watching him move smoothly while doing his thing,
Their eyes are focused searching for his wedding ring.

He has a style that is unlike any man around
With moves that take over any dance floor in town.

Doing moves that no one has ever seen,
As the women gather around and began to scream.

Something he has always dreamed to hear and feel
Dancing on the floor, it was just a thrill.

Enrolled in a local college seeking his degree,
Becoming a dancer was something he always wanted to be.

A doctor who studied to treat a serious illness
Something he does with compassion and skillness.

Another dream that is dear to his heart
As he struggles to keep these passions apart.

His days are filled with research to find a cure for cancer,
His nights with the desire to be a **Fancy Dancer.**

Fading Away

Day and night, they wonder about going their separate
ways. The reality of their hidden pain on full display.

Knowing their bodies are slowly fading away.
They will find a cure, some have faith to say.
Their hope appears darkened by the light of day.

Many are innocent victims of this deadly illness,
A hopeful life replaced by feelings of pure emptiness.

They fiercely hold on to the faith they have,
Some choose to cry while others find reasons to laugh.

Often feeling defeated in fighting this daily battle
Constantly hearing the death chains rattle.

AIDS is a disease that will cause the bravest to be afraid
Sadly, without protection, there are people out there
seeking to get laid.

A disease so deadly it can be bought with money,
Are you willing to give AIDS to your honey?

It can happen to anyone during a romantic night
Looking into the brightness of the moonlight.

Caught in the heat of the moment and led by the lust of
their flesh, as they help each other get undressed.

And at the end of that day they unknowingly begin to
Fade Away.

Dominos

Our life at times is like a million miles of fallen dominos
We quickly move through life falling as we go.

There is a clacking sound in the air
Someone has fallen who was once standing there.

As so many fall and that clacking sound enters our ear
We wonder who has fallen as the clacking sound draws near.

There are times in life when we are far above the ground,
Reach out and help someone who may have fallen down.

Because you never know when your domino may come
Tumbling around.

I Believe

I believe that your love is true.
I believe I am falling in love with you.

I believe that you sincerely care.
I believe in the life of love that we share.

I believe that the sun will always shine.
I believe in the dreams I have inside my mind.

I believe every word you whisper into my ear.
I believe you when you say I miss you my dear.

I believe that we will always be together.
I believe in our love lasting forever.

I believe in all the things you ever wanted me to be.
I believe in the dreams you shared with me.
I believe our life can be whatever we want it to be.

I believe it all started the moment I met you,
I believe whatever comes along we will make it through,
Because **I Believe** in you.

Where Is She?

The woman who shall be everything to me, Where Is
She? I've waited so long; I wonder where she could be.

The love that I have I will keep stored inside
Ready to be the one she calls to provide.

I know that she's out there somewhere
Filled with dreams of love looking for a man who cares.

I can't wait for the day that we finally meet,
A day my life will feel so complete.

I've had many thoughts of this day coming to pass
I wonder how long will these thoughts last.

Will I ever get the chance to experience real romance?
To hold her beautiful body close while we dance.

The thought of these moments often comes to mind
As each day goes by I search to find

The woman who would be all mine,
I can't find her, **Where Is She?**

Give Me Your Hand

Give me your hand and follow me into the light
There may be storms so hold on tight.

Give me your hand as we travel this way
Enjoying the beauty of another bright and sunny day.

Give me your hand and we will share the perfect love
Walking and holding hands counting the stars above.

Give me your hand to place upon my heart
To give me peace that I have desired from the start.

Give me your hand to hold in troubled times
I need to hold your hand to ease my troubled mind.

Give me your hand to remove my fears
To hold me close, wiping away my tears.

Give me your hand and I will be able to stand
At times I am weak I need to hold your hand.

Never to leave my side doing all that you can
I will find my way as long as I am holding your hand.

Waiting for You

I am standing! I am waiting! I am looking for you!
I see you, I feel you, but you are not there,
I can feel the texture of your long beautiful hair.

I hear strange voices speaking into my ear
I can feel your presence as these voices draw near.

Resting my eyes while blinking so often
I feel you touching me! Calling me! Pulling me!
I am searching for you! **Waiting for You,** so I wait.

My Girl

When I look at all of the things I am blessed with in the world, I begin to think of My Girl.

I open my window and look towards the sun
My mind is content as I think of the things we've done.

I can see the look on your face as I'm standing there
Reminiscing on the night I ran my fingers through your hair.

When you held my body close, my heart felt warm,
I wish you could have stayed until the break of dawn.

The love that we share is more valuable than all the money in the world. I feel so happy to have you as **My Girl.**

Thoughts For Our Love

Seasons come and seasons go
I hope one day to find a love that I will know.

Someone who can relieve my weary mind
And give me the peace that I have searched to find.

Inside I have so much I wish to share
I dream of finding that someone I know would truly care.

For compassion and hope I am willing to plant a seed
To find love is all I need.

I think of how wonderful it will be
You there witnessing such beauty with me.

Spring is near and the birds have begun to sing
I see a vision of this one special dream.

I am with someone that I've always loved
Watching the birds fly in the blue sky above.

The thought of love is here to stay
I've waited to love someone in a very special way.

I tried to hold this all inside
Not concerned with others, I have put away my pride.

These feelings I have must be from heaven above
In agreement with my **Thoughts for Our Love**.

This Time & The Last Time

This Time, I know that your love was true
I should have known it by all the things you tried to do.

The Last Time, I promised to make a change
Still, I lived my life just the same
 Leaving you all alone to carry the hurt and shame.

But This Time my heart is fixed
No longer am I playing selfish tricks.

The Last Time you said,
you'll never love again
And the guy you were with was just a friend.

I hope it is not too late to do all the things we planned
Remembering our first date when I held your hand.

I want to hear those special words again
When you said to me that I will always be your man

This time for the Last Time.

Our Lasting Love

The wind of life may continue to blow
The debts of our love only you and I know.

The rain may fall heavily on our face
 But the love we share will hold its place.

Difficult times in our life may occur
They will show that our love will remain secure.

Those times may cause us to be apart
 During those times I will keep you close to my heart.

The sun will always continue to shine
Long as we keep our lasting love in mind.

The fire in our love will forever burn
Your love for me will never be a concern.

It is not often that one can share this kind of love
You are a blessing that was given to me from above.

You show me just how much you really care
For our lasting love I know you will always be there.

Deborah Shedrick

Belong To You

Looking at the sky so beautiful and blue
I think of the days that I will spend with you.

They feel so real as the thoughts flow through my mind
I know our love is truly one of a kind.

I think of my life as a miracle with you
Each moment so special, as I think of all that we will do.

Being able to hold you fill my heart with gladness
Knowing no matter where I am
I can still feel your presence there.

To wrap my arms around you once again
To embrace and kiss you
Feeling the love growing within.

It all started when you became my friend
Falling in love, I felt it would never end.

I understand now why I fell for you
I know why I'm doing all the things I do.

It's all because of this precious gift of love
A gift that was sent from The Lord above.

A kind of love that is far overdue
I will always and forever **Belong To You**.

Masked Feelings

I hurt deep within my heart
Emotional, spiritual, perhaps I don't know where to start.

I smile as I mask all these feelings
While my life is being pulled away like banana peelings.

It appears as though I am in total control
The truth, I've hidden these things deep within my soul.

Hidden from a world I feel would not understand
Living my social life as a masked man.

I pray these burdens don't lead me to snap
And hit the ceiling before I get help for these malicious
Masked Feelings.

The Good Times and Bad Times

There are times in our lives when things are going well
When love has put us under a spell.

Wonderful thoughts flowing freely through our mind
These are clearly the good times.

There are days we feel weak searching for ways to be
strong. The troubles of life we are left to bear them alone,
We can agree these are the bad times.

There are times that are good and times that are bad
It is a part of life to be happy or sad.

We must reach inside and press our way
 Believing we will see a brighter day.

We may experience good times or bad times during our
day. They come, but remember they are not here to stay.

Whether it is good times or bad times we must be able to
stand. Always willing to reach out and offer someone a
helping hand.

Then Suddenly

There are moments in our life when we are
heading in the right direction
Every choice seems to be the right selection
Then Suddenly...

There are times when life is the best that we can
hope for it to be. A feeling that makes a captured
man feel free
Then Suddenly...

Enjoying a freedom that seems to have no end
Positioned with an opportunity to win
Then Suddenly...

Joy and peace standing firm and tall
Having a determined will to conquer all
Then Suddenly...

Adversity has proven your ability to win
Flourishing to have no end
Then Suddenly...

The brightness of the sun is present each passing
Day. The rain has been commanded to stay away
Then Suddenly...

Conditions in life are always on the verge of
Change. Creating a feeling that seems so strange
Then Suddenly...

Our lives at any moment could be subject to
Change. Our heart, mind and soul will never be the
Same. Leaving our lives filled with shame
Then Suddenly...

The Other Woman

You have caused me to feel a pain I've never experienced before, a pain I care not to ever feel any more.

Why! Tell me why! After all of these years
After building our marriage through blood, sweat and tears.

You allowed The Other Woman to tear our family apart
How can I tell our children! I don't know where to start.

She lied to you, telling you she knows how you feel
Convincing you that those feelings were real.

How could you believe her and do this to me?
She doesn't love you - Can't you see?
Does she know all we've been through?
I'm sure she doesn't have a clue.

After all I've done to help you get on your feet,
Is this my reward, you go out and cheat?

The pain I am feeling I did not see it coming
A pain you will soon feel from **The Other Woman**.

I'm Leaving You

I said that this would be your last time
I am tired of your cheating and lying.

You have scarred my mind, body and soul
By the many ways you managed to treat me cold.

You said time after time it would never happen again
And like a fool, I believed you and I let you back in.

I will not be making those same mistakes any longer
I have finally found someone who has made me stronger.

For the record, I have never lied nor cheated on you
On the other hand, it was something you'd often do.

You sold me dreams that you never tried to make come true. It is another reason I have made up my mind, I'm Leaving You!

You can never say that I did not show you love and respect. I had the opportunity to be with other men Instead, it was you that I chose to select.

Yes, I have suffered for making that regretful choice
Now I have my life back on the right course
With someone who has promised to be forever faithful and true
I will never be alone, although **I'm Leaving You**.

Your Beautiful Red Curly Hair

Many may look and they all may stare
But never mention Your Beautiful Red Curly Hair.

Bright as the sunlight
Shinning like the moon at night
With a smile that looks just right.

There are so many words you wish to say
Only having to look the other way.

But all the words you could ever share
Rest in the roots of
Your Beautiful Red Curly Hair.

I Love You

I love you for the happiness you bring my way
For all of the kind words you say each day.

I love you for the tenderness that lies within your heart
I love you for all you have given me from the very start.

I love you for your patience when I do something wrong
I love you for your laughter that lingers like a love song.

I love you for the gentle way you cheer me up when I am
sad. I love you for the little things you do to make my heart
glad.

I love you for the dreams you have shared with me
For the beauty of life you have helped me to see.

I love you for your smile that is so constant and true
But most of all, I love you just because you're you.

Friends Again

The days of our past have swiftly moved on their way. Looking back at pictures, remembering the kind words you would say.

Reminding me of the times you helped me to make it through. I haven't met a friend that compares to you.

Sometimes in a friendship one may disagree
While others see things the way it should be.

I never thought I would lose a friend so dear
There have been days when I wished you were here.

Your friendship gave me the strength to cope
Through all of my problems, your friendship gave me hope.

When I would feel down, you would find
a way to lift me up.

I still feel your kindness throughout each day
As I look to find the right words to say
Feeling your spirit guiding me as I travel along my
way.

I smell your fragrance traveling in the wind
It reminds me of how important it is for us to be
Friends Again.

Feelings

There are feelings of anger
Feelings that could lead us into danger.

Feelings of happiness and feelings of gladness
Feelings that bring about a sense of hope
Feelings that gives us the strength to cope.

Feelings of sadness mixed with madness
Feelings to share, feelings to care
Feelings of disappointments with feeling of despair.

Feelings of grace feelings of mercy
Feelings of laughter with feelings of loneliness
Feelings of winning and feelings of loosing
Feelings of giving, feelings of taking.

Feelings to live and feelings to die
Feelings of truth and feelings to lie.

Feelings of love and feelings of hate
What are your feelings?
Take a few moments and meditate.

I Believe

I believe that your love is true
I believe I am falling in love with you.

I believe that you sincerely care
I believe in the life of love that we share.

I believe that the sun will always shine
I believe in the dreams I have inside my mind.

I believe every word you whisper into my ear
I believe you when you say I miss you my dear.

I believe that we will always be together
I believe in our love lasting forever.

I believe in all the things you ever wanted me to be
I believe in the dreams you shared with me
I believe our life can be whatever we want it to be.

I believe it all started the moment I met you
I believe whatever comes along we will make it through
Because, **I Believe** in you.

Why Am I?

Why am I falling so deeply in love with you?
Laughing, dreaming, then crying and regretting
The things we do.

Why am I running as though I am in a race?
To feel your warm and tender embrace
My heart pounding as I look into your face.

Why am I walking away from everything I own?
Feeling content as we dance to our love song.

Why am I believing in a love I know will soon end?
Knowing you are married to my best friend.

Why am I? Why am I? Finding myself doing this?
Again and again, Why?

Deborah Shedrick

My Soul Mate

The very moment I laid eyes on you, I knew you would
be my wife. The woman I have been searching for all my of
life.

Someone who would help me overcome life's fears
And help to dry up my falling tears.

The power of love I am still trying to understand
As I go on learning how to become a man.

You bring out parts of me that I never knew
As I find myself falling deeper in love with you.

Your tender voice and your beautiful smile keeps me
mesmerized. Seeing the presence of love each time I look
into your eyes.

A feeling that causes me to get weak in my knees
A feeling so refreshing, it's like a cool summer breeze.

Your kiss is sweet with a touch of splendor
Each time you hold me it causes me to surrender.

It makes me want to scream out and tell the world
I have found a treasure one priceless pearl!

Someone that I dare my love to hesitate
I am happy and content in finding you, **My Soul Mate**.

I Am A Woman

I am a woman that is strong
I am a woman who does not wish to live my life alone.

I am a woman who understands
I am a woman that will support and respect her man.

I am a woman who knows the meaning of love
I am a woman who will stick closer than a hand in a glove.

I am a woman who is independent, alive and free
I am a woman who knows the importance of a family.

I am a woman who shows that she care
I am a woman, If you need me I'll be there.

A Godly Wife

God created the woman before man sinned
To be his helpmate, lover and his friend
His companion in a dire time of need
A woman who would later bring forth God's holy seed
Someone who all mankind would one day need.

To be his comfort whenever he is feeling alone
Helping to keep her man strong
A Godly wife adds meaning to an ordinary day
Her husband quietly stands watching while she prays.

Her love flows from the inside out
Possessing a kind of love that is never in question or doubt
She has a way of making her husband feel like a king
Being his wife, his joy, and every waking dream.

Her support and encouragement helps him believe he
can as she stands strong and brave beside her man
Who is like this woman here on Earth
Someone who has so willingly given all of us birth.

 She helps her man through the many challenges of life
As he deals with all types of danger and strife
How important is it to have a **Godly Wife.**

The Blackness In You

Candy Productions

You are a beautiful black woman that brings brightness to the darkest of night. You are a woman that a man would consider his delight.

For your family you demonstrate a strong will to fight. Willing to change any of their wrongs into right.

Seeing you truly stirs my mind, body and soul
You bring a warmth I need in a world that has been so cold.

Releasing love that causes me to lose all self-control
Reaching for any part of your body I can hold.

Your style weakens a strong willed man
The moment he feels the warm touch of your hand
Regardless of the resistance, it will fail to stand.

You are a precious and priceless treasure,
Blessed beyond any measure.

You are a black woman that is capable of making
The dreams of your man come true
Something that you have been known to do.

The world have always fallen weak for the strength, the beauty and **The Blackness In You**.

Addiction

Addiction has claimed the lives of many
Stripping away their hopes and dreams down to their last
penny.

Addiction has caused the deaths of both the rich and poor
Many are suffering while locked behind a prison door.

They are people just like you and I
Why can't we hear their painful cry?

They are people with problems you may not understand
We should love them enough to direct them to someone
who can.

Giving them the chance to get their life back on track
To help relieve their struggles from this disease vicious
attack.

The effect of Addiction we see in our communities
And on our city block. We ask ourselves the question,
why can't they just stop?

They are in need of your support and hugs to give them
renewed hope. Something that replaces the comfort they
seek when doing their dope.

Brooke Winn, Oh Beetlebum

Cocaine Pain

He started with a local band where he played and sang
With hopes of making him a very big name.

He would play his guitar and bring life to any bar
After closing, he would still entertain
Sitting on the hood of his old car.

He never smoked nor drank any kind of booze
Straight into the big times he was destined to cruise.

He would say, "Man I'm not going to stop
Until I reach the billboard chart."

Until then I'll keep playing until I drop
Grabbing his guitar drinking the last of a soda pop.

One night as he played there was a girl in the crowd
Dancing to his music and singing out loud.

He grabbed her hand pulling her up on stage
A few weeks later they were engaged.

No one knew from where this girl came
Not to speak of hearing mention of her name.

Only recalling the night she got on stage and sang
Some say it was a downright shame
When she got him into the cocaine game.

Today his music is memories of the past
As he sit on an old porch with whiskey in his glass.

Another bright and talented future of success and fame
Now converted into a man on the verge of going insane.

Left to suffer in a life of **Cocaine Pain**.

Recovery

We enter into recovery far before we know
Tired of the pain, still unable to let the substance go.

We seem to be lost unable to find our way out
While so many stand by filled with disappointment and doubt.

We struggle to gain hours and days of clean time
Anything that would help ease our clouded mind.

In search of a life that brings happiness and peace
Feelings and emotions that we can now release.

Something that was once lost inside of me
Only to be found when I embraced the life of **Recovery**.

Not In Vain

In life you may experience moments of sadness
There will be days that you feel joy and gladness.

You may be faced with sickness and pain
Christ has assured us that it is not in vain.

Your day may be dark, the skies filled with the presence of
gray. You can rest in assurance of the glory of
Christ returning one day.

Throughout the days of living this life
Whether in the spirit of peace or at times in strife.

Remember Jesus has given us hope in His name
That whatever we go through it is **Not In Vain.**

RONALD M. BALDWIN

The Death Rope

They were brought to America with no dreams of
prosperity or hope.
For many generations they were threatened by the death
rope.

Forced into being servants of all kinds laboring
In some cotton field.
Having their spiritual songs and prayers were their only
shield.

Grieved but knew they had to survive
It was the only way their dreams could come alive.

In spite of the fear of being hung from the death rope,
They were determined to maintain their vision of hope.
Giving them the will to be able to cope.

The death rope claimed an unknown number of BLACK
AMERICAN lives during that heartless and brutal slavery
Time.
Some of those horrible memories are still trapped
inside their mind.

Still, there are those whose heart and mind refuse to change.

Evil and hatred still running strong within their veins.

Proudly flying their hate flag and screaming out White Hope, holding high in the air their threatening symbol of **The Death Rope.**

Game Over

Cell 204

It all began when I was just a teenager
I purchased my first package, a cell phone and a pager.

Clients would call and arrangements were set
I never could imagine it would be one that I'll regret.

I purchased name brand clothes and flashy jewelry
Drove some of the finest cars one could want to see
Feeling confident that no one could ever touch me.

I became comfortable as I rose to the top of the drug game
Having clubs, the fine women, a home and plenty of fame.

I later decided to expand
I felt I was gaining the upper hand.

I planned a high level meeting
When I entered the room and gave my formal
greeting.

I heard a loud knock and a crashing sound
Voices screaming out and guns drawn.

Ordering us to get on the ground. Game Over!
Now, I'm smarter and much older.

I find myself thinking of the foolish mistakes I made over the years. My eyes begin to fill with tears.

Listening to the sound as they fall to the concrete floor
Realizing there will never be any room service for the man behind the door in **Cell 204.**

Lost Black Men

Deborah Shedrick

Every day that goes by we are losing a record number of our men.

They seem to be vanishing like the chaff blowing in the wind.

Who would be a better role model for a son other than His father and friend?

Our jails and prisons are on the verge of a total overflow
The numbers continue to rise, to where, who could ever
know?

When a black male that is brought up without his father
It makes it harder for that child to cope
He enters into manhood with little or no hope.

Sadly, many of these young men are seen loitering
Day and night on any city street
Any day we could witness a crime scene
With another black man lying beneath a sheet.

Many of these men find themselves living a life of crime
Only to be arrested at any given time.

Charged and convicted stuck inside "The Pen"
Added to the long and endless list of
A society of **Lost Black Men.**

Drum Majors

Who is willing to face the real challenges of this new
generation?

While some experience real freedoms, sadly some
Still have their minds stuck on some plantation.

Today our slave owners no longer carry a whip
Nor do they transport slaves in a ship.

They have no need to hide under a hooded sheet
Because today's slave owners are the destructive things
We so willingly drink, smoke, and eat.

These slave owners openly trade one slave for another
Trading in markets that are more brutal than any other.
A market that destroys the hopes and dreams of
our black sisters and brothers.

Why have we allowed these slaves owners to invade our
land? After so many have marched and died
So we could become a respected woman or man.

Many of the leaders who stood firm and strong are gone
Leaving us with slim hope of ever hearing another soul
stirring Negro freedom song.

Many of our new generations are content with using or
dealing drugs.
While others are on our streets wanting to become thugs.

There are those who are focused on attending college
Determined to obtain a degree of knowledge.

Our nation is in need of the new generation teenagers
With a burning desire to become
One of our heroic **Drum Majors**.

RONALD M. BALDWIN

The New Orleans Blues

Famous for Jazz, Cajun Food and dancing to the sounds of the Blues. Nearly deserted with only memories while in search for clues.

Many unanswered questions continue to plague the people's mind. Visions still fresh of the faces of those who were suffering and dying.

Memories that will forever cause tears to fall and hearts become quite heavy. Remembering the powerful rushing waters that were released from the broken levees.

One of the many questions that troubled our Nation's mind. As we look at a city that appears to be lost in a perilous time.

Unknown numbers of people are either missing or dead While others are in search to make sure their families are fed.

People who were once filled with the energy of life
Dancing to the sounds of Jazz and Blues far into the night
The hope for those joyous times returning seems nowhere
in sight.

Katrina washed the lives and dreams of so many away
With her powerful winds of destruction on that dark,
stormy day. Leaving behind thousands searching for a safe
place to stay.

Forced to live with the horrible memories of death,
desperation, hunger and pain. Some packed up and left,
while others were determined to maintain.

The thought of giving up those "Marching Saints"
downright refused. Never will they give up The City of
Jazz and **The New Orleans Blues.**

Slave Graves

Way out yonder in the right corner of this old cotton field
Is where my grandpa and grandma were brutally killed.

The smell of their blood seemed to be fresher this time
Around. As generations of our family silently stand as
their tears fall to the ground.

What a degrading way in which they died
Stories have been told that grandpa just got tired.

He was fed up with the life of working in a cotton field
Tired of doing his slave master's will.

A man of integrity who lived his life upright
The sound of the slave master's whip was heard
throughout the night. It was told that grandpa put up a
hell of a fight.

Grandma tried relentlessly to get them to stop!
The stains of her blood still on the ground where she fell
after being shot!

Who is content with being a slave on a cotton field?
A life that will one day cause them to be killed.

I can hear the sound of my grandpa's voice
Pleading for this generation to make the right choice.

To wipe away all their tears
To stand strong and face your fears.

A choice that will cause your life to be saved
Setting your soul free from a cold and lonely
Slave Grave.

Who Truly Cares?

Brooke Winn, Oh Beetlebum

So many of us are being left behind, without living a full life. Forced to live in a world filled with trouble and strife.

With wars, destruction, disease and countless natural disasters unfolding unaware. The poor and homeless we often see everywhere
To simply walk in our city streets has become a total scare.

The mentally ill, deaf and dumb and elderly they don't stand a chance. The handicapped are not strong enough to take a stance.

Some mothers or fathers walk out, leaving a child in a world of the unknown
Leaving them to grow up on their own.

Love and compassion seems to have vanished out of the hearts and minds of many
While they enjoy their lives filled with plenty.

There are those who possess wealth by the millions
 Having stocks and bonds and many corporate shares
They have become well known billionaires.

Seriously ask yourself this important question,
Who Truly Cares?

The Shameful Rich

There are so many people who don't dream anymore
Seeing the rich become richer and the poor remain poor
We see people who are starving everywhere
Then we hear of someone becoming a millionaire.

Many poor people struggle to have a meal to eat
Some die trying from the extreme cold or heat
While millionaires fly high above in a first class seat.

Selfishness and greed have taken a grip on some of the
rich around the world. What has happened to the
compassion we once had for the hungry boy or girl?

Have those caring and loving thoughts been erased from
our mind. Some apparently don't care and refuse to be
kind. Content in seeing another poor person dying.

Still, television ads and billboards we see everywhere
Pleading for anything that any of us would be willing to
spare.

Another urgent and desperate humanitarian sales
pitch. Designed to reach inside the hearts of
The Shameful Rich.

Closed Eyes

Why can't you see the millions starving around the world? Perhaps you are blinded by your diamonds and pearls.

Why can't you see the troubled young boy
Who desire is to have his favorite toy?

His father has never been present in the home
He spends his days and nights all alone.

Why can't you see the constant rise of youth crime?
Could you be a victim the next time?
Could this be the only way some speak their mind?

Why can't you see the pain on a homeless person face?
They don't need your money - only your embrace.

Why can't we love and care for one another?
After all, we are all sisters and brothers

If this is something you can't come to realize
Maybe, it is because you have **Closed Eyes**.

Ronnie Phillips

Wife Beater

They come from all types of ethnic backgrounds
Beating on their wives from sun up to sun down.

They are hidden deep within our society
They come in every variety.

Cleverly they manage to hide behind their cowardly acts
Turning up the heat during their brutal attacks.

With the desire to tame their wives as you would a dog
Often leaving their victims bloody and in a mental fog.

We wonder why these men chose to take this route
Was this how they were taught to let their frustrations
out?

Could it be that they are a controlling cheater?
One who has become a **Wife Beater?**

A King Who Defiles Our Black Queens

My Brothers, My Brothers! Have you lost your kingship
minds?
It appears as though you are willing to treat our
Black Queens worse than the white man did back during
the heartless slavery times.

Why have you chosen this disrespectful role?
Taking our Black Queens treating them so dishonorable
and cold.

Where did you learn this type of behavior?
Have you forgotten all their struggles, sacrifices and
labor?

Is it the greed of the mighty dollar that has taken your
mind there? Taken you to a place that has caused you not
to care.

The words used towards our "Black Queens" is far from
the dream of our honorable, Dr. King.
I am sure those words were not a part of his dream.

Regain your integrity my brother!
Our Black Queens should not have to look to any other.

We are the watchman over their precious heart and mind
Not to be the one that treats them unkind.

Brothers, brothers, where is your strength, morals and
pride? Show the world that you are willing and capable of
standing respectfully by her side.

No longer being ashamed of the many past unjust things
Because now, you are no longer
A King Who Defiles Our Black Queens.

I Am Sorry

I Am Sorry
I didn't tell you how you made me feel
How I enjoyed every moment, your love was such
a thrill.

I Am Sorry
For all the foolish things I did to break your heart
My life hasn't been the same since we've been
apart.

I wonder if I will ever again, hold your hand
I wonder if we will ever play on the beach in the
sand.

I can still hear your voice as you call my name
How could I've been so foolish, I feel so ashamed.

It hurt me to even think on all the things we have
done
How you would smile, I knew you were having fun

Then, I do something so foolish and hurt the one I
love
Please forgive me, because... **I Am Sorry.**

Losing My Mind Over You

Am I insane for bearing the pain that you keep putting
me through? The last time, I promised myself I was
finished with you.

Again, I am heartbroken still holding on to you
Asking myself what in the world am I going to do?

I have thought about leaving to somehow get over you
Where would I go? I haven't a clue
Wherever I go my heart will always be with you.

As I stand in the rain with my luggage in my hand
Trying to convince myself to become a stronger man.

Still unable to stop my heart from screaming out your
name. Wondering whether or not I am truly going insane.

I am trying to figure out what to do
Wondering if I am on the verge of
Losing My Mind Over You.

In Time You'll See

You have always been someone very dear to me,
The promises I made they will forever be.

I know at times you needed me and I wasn't there
My actions appeared as if I really didn't care
I did things according to my own selfish will
Treating you wrong seemed to me as no big deal.

During those times I kept so much inside
Feelings I felt that I needed to hide
I look back on the times you smiled when you should have
cried. Accepting things as truth knowing that I had lied.

You did it all just to be there for me
With the hope that your love would somehow set me free
You are the best woman that I ever had
Please forgive me for all the times I made you sad.

Our life together and all of our dreams
I will give to you with many other special things
It happened because of the love you gave to me
And I will do the same **In Time You'll See.**

Trust and Love

There are many who say that they are in love
But do they share trust as a flock of precious doves?
They feel content when their minds are clear
As long as the one they love is happily standing near.

Thoughts of mistrust when they are apart
Begin to beat upon their heart
We wonder in our mind whether their love is true
Most of the time it's based on the things that they say or
do.

For the sake of love we put trust in the one we are with
While spending valuable time, buying them expensive
gifts. We feel that these actions will somehow build trust
remembering the power of our own uncontrollable lust.

In a relationship where love is true
Whether they are in your presence or far away from you
Always respect them with Trust and Love in all you do
because they could be that someone who is truly in love
with you.

My Precious Flower

You are like a beautiful blossom
that blooms at the beginning
Of a new Spring Season
Being with you is so warm and pleasing.

I am in need of your love every passing hour
I find myself falling head over heels for you
My Precious Flower.

When you became a part of my world
I changed the way I think and live
You have shown why someone who is in love
Should learn to forgive.

When the burdens of life weigh heavy on my heart
I find comfort when I reflect on how my life was from our
Start. So if my days are sunny and bright
Or with a forecast of an evening shower.

I find much comfort in knowing
I'll be able to share those moments
With you, **My Precious Flower**.

Is It Love?

When love moves at a steady pace
As if it is running in a race
And someone doesn't give you space
Is it love?

If you are in a place where love is excelling
The thought of love causes your heart to start swelling
Is it love?

If there are plans that seem so bright
Happiness beaming like the sunlight
Is it love?

I have been feeling this way for a while
Each morning I open my eyes these thoughts make me
smile.

I never want these feelings to disappear
Feelings that seem all so clear
Is it love?

Candy Productions

Dream Walking

Walking along the shore you and I
With love sparkles in both of our eyes
Playing along the beach in the sand
As we walk hand and hand.

Each step that we took my heart began to pound
My mind started to race when you let your hair down
We ended up on the shore far from where we started
I never felt so light hearted.

You pulled me close as we watched the moon come into
Sight. You asked if I would hold you like this every night
The softness of your kiss I felt upon my face
Your hand moving gently along my waist.

It was a night of love filled with passion
Moving to the sound of the waves splashing

I will never forget the day we started talking
And since that day, I have been **Dream Walking**.

I'll Be There

I knew the day would come that you would have to go
The sadness I now have I never wanted to know.

My heart will always be with you no matter how long you
stay. I know our love will find each other again someday.

So if you need someone to call that surely cares
If you need a shoulder to cry on, mine I would spare.

When the burdens of life begin and you are many miles
away. My love will fly like a bird in the spring to brighten
your darkest day.

Remember that these times may only be a test
To make our love its very best.

Something that I will always be willing to share
Letting you know that **I'll Be There**.

Are You Alright?

As I lie here in bed on this cold winter's night
Thinking about our love, wondering if it is all right
I feel deep inside the presence of fear
Hoping I don't lose a love that is so very dear.

My spirit cries out for your tender touch
You know that I love you so very much
You are not here for me to tell
My mind stands still as if I'm under a spell.

I feel that I am in a small world all alone
Searching for ways to keep our love strong
There are moments that I struggle throughout each day
For our love I will always pray.

I know my life would not be the same without you
I think of all the days that your love saw me through

I cherish each thought that enters into my mind
To share them with you in due time

Now as I lie here holding my pillow tight
A thought comes to mind I'm wondering
Are You Alright?

Living Without You

Slowly the days, months, and years have drifted by
Lying in my cold and lonely bed about to cry
Unclear of the reasons why.

I guess it was because I have never experienced the power
of love with anyone the way I have with you
Imagining without it what in the world would I do?

I cherish those special moments we've been blessed to
share. Each day you are away makes it harder for me to
bear.

I find some relief whenever I hold your picture close to my
Heart. Feeling your presence even though we're many
miles apart.

Falling in love with you has transformed a life I once lived
in vain. A life filled with bad relationships, disappointments
and pain.

I feel truly blessed to have met someone like you
From the very moment I saw you I just knew
My life would be nearly impossible **Living Without You.**

I Care

When life seems hard and there is no one there,
remember, I Care

When you feel so alone and you can't be strong know that
I Care

Whenever you need someone to hold and whisper words
untold, I Care

When love seems to be so far away and you desire to
have a love that will always stay, remember these words
that I now share

I will forever be there because
I Care.

Don't Cry

Don't cry because I have decided to leave
I've asked you not to carry your feelings and emotions
on your sleeve.

Your past relationship has caused you to be love scared
I have tried to show you how much I really cared.

You rejected everything that real love is about
Placing yourself in a state of love doubt.

Why can't you just understand; Look at me!
I am not that other man!

You said that he lied and was never true
Since we met I have tried to prove how much I love you.

Something you will not accept and I clearly understand
the reasons why.
Reasons that have led me to finally say goodbye.

Still, I will always love you, so please baby
Don't cry.

Friends Again

The days of our past have swiftly moved on their way,
 Looking back at pictures, remembering the kind words
you would say.

Reminding me of the times you helped me to make it
through. I haven't met a friend that compares to you.

Sometimes in a friendship one may disagree
While others see things the way it should be.

I never thought I would lose a friend so dear
There have been days when I wished you were here.

Your friendship gave me the strength to cope
Through all of my problems, your friendship gave me
hope. When I would feel down, you would find a way to
lift me up.

I still feel your kindness throughout each day
As I look to find the right words to say
Feeling your spirit guiding me as I travel along my way.

I smell your fragrance traveling in the wind
It reminds me of how important it is for us to
Be Friends Again.

RONALD M. BALDWIN

Alonzo McNeal, Picture Perfect

I Fly High

I fly high above into the blue sky in search of a place to
nest and rest.

Spreading my wings, determined to fly at
my very best.

In search of a place to rest my weary wings
A place where I can live out all my dreams
While listening to the songs that the birds sing.

A place that is refreshing and pleasing
Somewhere I can go to enjoy all four seasons
While discovering my life purpose and reasons.

I have flown many times not knowing where to go
Seeing the beauty of life far in the distance below.

I fly with confidence as I soar into the sky
Stretching my wings, joining in as the birds sing
I Fly High

The Wind

The wind blows all around us, but no one knows where the wind goes.

The wind moves the leaves on our trees and the waves on our seas, but no one knows where the wind blows.

Life is like the wind that blows and no man knows where life really goes.

Life is all around us just like the wind
And there is no life without a friend.

Just notice the birds how they trust the wind
You can say The Wind is their friend.

At Dawn

At Dawn I still see the presence of the night
The stars in the sky shinning bright with the moon in sight.

Dawn is the beginning of a brand new day
My body lies still as my mind quickly moves away.

I think of all the things that have happened the day before
Some thoughts make my heart happy while others make it sore.

Today's trials and tribulations are fresh inside my mind
I'll know if I'll have the victory within due time.

As the moon disappears slowly and the stars fade away
The sun begins to rise as I start this new day.

I wonder in my mind concerning how this day will be
And whether or not it is the last sunrise I will see.

I then see the moon move into place
As the sunlight goes down and night takes its space
I find myself again awake **AT DAWN.**

Sounds of the Sea

Alonzo McNeal, Picture Perfect

As I stand listening to the sounds of the sea
I can imagine what each sound means to me.

Seeing the seagulls flying gracefully through the air
Feeling the wind as it blows through my hair.

I am so relaxed, I am feeling so free, as I stand here
listening to the **Sounds of the Sea.**

Summer Breeze

Today the sunrise is much more meaningful than before
As I stand staring out my front door.

I hear birds as they began to sing
Flying so freely with outstretched wings.

I see the leaves as they move gracefully on the trees
I open my door I am emotionally pleased.
Feeling truly bless to feel another **Summer Breeze**.

Beauty Burners

They are out there anxiously waiting to see one of their
fires flare. If anyone is killed they more than likely
wouldn't care.

They are thrilled to see the fire and smoke
everywhere. Watching the determined efforts of the fire
fighters on the ground and in the air.

Wild life is being forced out of their rightful habitation
Homes are being destroyed while the owners are on
vacation.

Miles and miles of beautiful forest going up in smoke
And a Beauty Burner thinks that it's some kind of joke.

The environment is vital to our life span
So help take the matches out of their hands

Become a part of those who are environmentally
concerned.

Aimed to stop the destruction caused by those
who enjoy watching our beautiful forest burn.

Rainy Day

Yesterday was so sunny and my smile was bright
A day I'll never forget, things seemed so right.

Love moved all through the air
I felt that I finally found someone who cares
I thought of all the things in life you and I would
share when the storms of life come we'll both be
able to bare.

Many days I desired to see your face
I recall you saying it was love that you wanted to
embrace.

I tried many times to reach you by phone
But each time I called I received a busy tone.

Then, one sunny day as I went on my way
I saw you and her standing there; I didn't know
what to say.

The sun in my life suddenly went away
Once again, it was another **Rainy Day.**

The Sea Shore

Alonzo McNeal, Picture Perfect

The crashing waves speak so loudly to my soul
Surrendering my emotions under a Supreme control.

Standing on The Sea Shore in search of a peace of mind
A place I visit frequently during my troubled times.

Seeing the sun rise I try to make sense
Of the things in life that cause me to be so tense.

Life seems to be much less of an endless chore
As I stand peacefully alone on **The Sea Shore**.

The Leaf

I saw a special leaf upon a tree
That one leaf meant so much to me
Each day that I passed under the tree
That one special leaf would inspire me.

The sun would shine and the rain would pour
The wind would blow
But The Leaf held on even more.

One autumn evening as I passed by
The Leaf fell into my path and I knew why.

The Leaf showed me how strong I can be
How to bare the storms of life that would come upon me
I will always have this story to tell
About the day when The Leaf fell.

For Love Too

Love has always been for life and life is to love
The message God gave when He sent Jesus from above.

Love has meaning far more than anyone of us may ever
know. His love goes further than anyone of us would be
willing to go, to the height of the heavens far beyond the
depths of the ocean floor.

The power of His love reaches as far as the east is from the
west. This Godly love will always perform at its best
Leading a weary mind into a peaceful and soothing rest.

His love is reliable, firm and strong
Discovering reasons to keep holding on

God's love would never leave room for doubt or fear
Are you willing to make your love that crystal clear?
For Love Too

Why I Sing

I sing to bring my mind into a place of rest
To ease the pressures of life that weigh upon my chest

I sing out loud because my sadness is deep
The words I sing were once hidden far beneath.

Far beneath the smiles I carry through my day
Each song I sing help direct my way

I sing to myself during the rough times
 I sing to help ease my weary mind.

I sing because I see what you are going through
I sing hoping to somehow reach you
That is **Why I Sing**.

A Dear Friend

Today I am grateful to have you in my life
Someone that helps me make all of my wrongs right.

A person who has proven to show me endless love
Just as God did when He sent Jesus from above.

Your friendship will forever mean the world to me
Whenever I am in need of a true friend it is your face that
I see.

Thank you so much for being A Dear Friend to me.

The Cross

For centuries there has been The Cross
Memories of that day could never be lost

The Cross is displayed around the globe
Its meaning to man continues to unfold.

The Cross is often seen
The bearer is the Creator of everything

He shed His blood for the sins of the world
To offer salvation to every woman, man, boy and girl.

Countless people wear The Cross
I wonder if they are saved or if they are lost

The purpose is not always clear
The important thing is they have The Cross near.

Some have said they have it for their protection
 Others have said they wear it for direction

Their thoughts and reasons appear to be true
 But let me make it clear Jesus came and died for you
on **The Cross**.

Life

Alonzo McNeal, Picture Perfect

Life is to be lived according to the Lord
The chances we take we cannot afford

We should live our life showing kindness and meekness
Never willing to take advantage of anyone's weakness.

Instead of hatred and confrontation
We should show love and consideration

Life can be beautiful, as many of us have seen
We all have an opportunity to fulfill our dream.

There are those who choose to live a hateful life
Through envy and vengeance that cuts like a knife

The degree of conflict in this life we often see
Holds our spirit captive not allowing it to be free.

We only get one earthly opportunity to live
Love and happiness we should all be willing to give

Showing love and kindness to everyone as we go
Because the end of one's Life, no one will ever know.

ABOUT THE AUTHOR

Ronald M. Baldwin Sr. was inspired by the late **James Baldwin**, American Novelist, poet and writer of similar subject matter – that of controversy and truth.

Born in Portsmouth, Virginia to Naval Chief Petty Officer Daniel James and Betty L. Baldwin, Ronald is the sixth of nine children all born on the East Coast. Orders from the United States Navy relocated the family to Pensacola, Florida where the father retired after serving 30 years.

After attending grade school and graduating from high school in Pensacola, Florida, his dream to serve his country as his father did came to fruition. Ronald served three years in the United States Army and although a short military career, he learned countless life lessons and began to write about his everyday life experiences in the form of poetry. He writes about subjects everyone can relate to and subject matters pertaining to the challenges of life – love, political, spirituality, and personal life issues.

Ronald's desire is that his work will stir the mind, heart, and soul of the reader. His poetry will help you enjoy, relate and embrace the challenges we face in our ever changing society.

Contact Ronald Baldwin

ronaldbaldwin909@gmail.com
Facebook - RMBdeepVoice

VOICES

Made in the USA
Middletown, DE
07 June 2023

31881373R00096